Threading Raindrops

Michele Fermanis-Winward

Threading Raindrops

Acknowledgements

I thank Deb Westbury for her generous mentoring and editorial skills;
the Siding Poets and Writers, Vanessa Kirkpatrick, Brendan Doyle,
Kathy Hale, Emma Brazil, Tom Williams and John Lekkas,
for their friendship and advice, creating an environment
where this book could be realised;
Brown's Siding Café at Medlow Bath for their hospitality;
Kathy Gerontakos and Paul Thiering for continued wise counsel;
and Hannah Terkes and James Paull at Gleebooks, Blackheath,
for their encouragement and enthusiasm for the written word.

With love and gratitude to my friends and family for their unstinting
love and support; they inspired many of the poems in this collection.

Poems in this collection have previously appeared in *Eureka Street*,
Blackmail Press (NZ), *Blue Fringe 'Celebrating Life'*
and *Narrator* magazine.

Dedicated to my husband Kevin
and my brothers James and Peter

Threading Raindrops
ISBN 978 1 74027 904 8
Copyright © Michele Fermanis-Winward 2015

First published 2015 by
GINNINDERRA PRESS
PO Box 3461 Port Adelaide 5015 Australia
www.ginninderrapress.com.au

Contents

First Thoughts	7
The Pond	8
Unencumbered Days	10
Housework	11
He Loves to Shop	12
Heartbeats	13
The Ear	14
Out There	15
Keeping to the Line	16
Poetic Cooling	17
Found Wanting	18
Illusion	19
Metalworking	20
After the Funeral	21
Powerless	22
Her Laughter	23
Trying	24
Brother	25
Behind Locked Doors	26
Icarus	27
The Game	28
History	29
Laos	30
Drones	32
Running	33
What Cannot Be Contained	34
Rot and Weeds	35
White Stone Blades	36
Solitary Confinement	37
Storm Thrush	38

Unseasonal	39
The Summer House	40
Reflecting on Monet	41
Blended in Blue	43
Whale Watching	44
After the Storm	45
Coastal	46
Coolum Morning	47
At Port	48
Calligraphy	49
Shipwrecked	50
Teasing	51
Painting Lives	52
The Quiet	53

First Thoughts

I wake to words,
the dancing syllables of sound
spin in my head,
lines form, dissolve and rearrange,
stop me
from skiving underneath the quilt,
abandon the lover at my side,
insist I drag a body stiff with sleep
and stagger down the hall,
find dressing gown, fight slippers onto feet.

Lights switch,
the work of yesterday
shoved to one side,
outside the sky suffused in pink.
There are stray notes
of bowerbirds and currawongs,
on the prowl.
Like them I'm up for early worms,
to fuel my flight in verse.

The Pond

I rush towards my new retreat
its paths and banks
impose a measured step
upon my racing mind.

Fronds unfurl
and shafts of bracken rise
within the half-light
overhung with trees.

My finger traces whorls and curves
dark spikes erect and leathery
or feather heads of maidenhair
on legs of apple green,
trembling in my hand.

My back against
a lichen rasp of cherry tree,
the dance will not begin
until I can be still.
Here time is seasonal.

Minutes pass,
water snails emerge
promenade on strands of watercress,
nibble frogs' eggs, floating roots,
explore the herbs I spread.

Emerging from a bed
of rounded stones
a solitary leech stands and waves
towards my warmth.
I'm mesmerised,
admire its pinstriped elegance.
The fish remain unseen.

Above my head an olive bowerbird
cries its harsh alarm.
My eyes return to skim the pond.

I glimpse a flash of speckled red
the shimmer I am waiting for.
In gold and silver costuming
the ballet now begins.

Without a noise or shadow fall
I watch the fish perform.
Arabesque between the plants,
their *pas de deux*
dissolves my sense of time.

Unencumbered Days

From rising to resting
when you can ignore
the dishes, the dusting
and washing on the floor.

No phone calls to answer
or knock on the door,
no one about you
whose needs must go before.

Your own precious hours
just to dream and draw.
From morning to midnight
I wish that there were more.

Housework

I fold the clothes
and mop the sticky floor.
Memories long buried
knock gently in my head.

Love was often scalding
till passion had been spent.
But loss is less corrosive
when watered down by time.

My heart at last is mended
upon the pile of years.
This effort spent in cleaning
no longer feels a chore.

He Loves to Shop

Inhaling through a Tim Tam
clenched to stifle rage
at time's black hole misspent
in the labyrinth of shelves.

His list was short,
goods to be found
elusive as our summer days,
frogs croaking in a drought.

Their game it seems,
is to rearrange
from top to bottom shelf,
or move them somewhere else.

He finds a labelled youth
who vaguely shrugs,
points him to an aisle
he's searched three times before.

Resolving now to do without,
he heads for comfort food,
the fuel he needs
to get him past the checkout queue.

At home, one item out of date
another turning green,
Tim Tam breathing brings relief,
as empty wrappers hit the bin.

Heartbeats

The clock that ticks within
will sometimes go awry
and turn time upside down.
The pulse
which kept your life
revolving on its course
had jammed beneath the skin.

Dread of what this meant
has frozen all our schemes.
Your light upon my days
had threatened to go out.
To leave my face a blank
with hands that will not move.

The Ear

Curled as a burning leaf,
it cups our lives,
a portal to the world of noise,
frames laughter, songs and cries,
incites or soothes our rage.

Love expressed in whispers
is shared in closed embrace.
We sift and weigh our value through
cacophonies of years.
Step from the maze inside our heads,
clasp until the end,
a voice we hold most dear.

Out There

Woken by some unfamiliar sound
I'm waiting.
Seconds become a universe.
I enter deep space
planets spin, stars die
a black hole of fright swallows my sleep.
Imagination flashes, a comet
trailing violent possibilities.
I'm trapped in Terra Mortis
straining to hear beyond its darkness.
My heart beating out of my body
ricochets off the walls
panic tracing an arced orbit across my mind
I'm waiting – in the quiet – I am waiting.
Time drifts, weightless
until the gravity of exhaustion
pulls me down to sleep.
I splash back
into another haggard day.

Keeping to the Line

I hang on the line
connected to reality,
repeat each day,
repair stray threads.
This work demands
its pattern to be tight.

Sun strikes illuminate
an intricate design,
strength held inside a strand
the pride in what's been spun.
I jump,
defy the filament's extent
into unknown terrain.

New traps are set for life,
the years crossed out
like captured moths,
my trophies in decay
that spin upon the web.

Poetic Cooling

My head stews in its stock of words,
verbs grow hot,
stanzas sweat for want of rest.
I must concede they're lost,
stand up and look for respite,
repeating lines by hand.

Disgorge the boxes where I hoard
my stash of wools in colour-indexed rows.
Resharpen with emery
two spikes of cherry wood.
Looped threads around stiff fingers
will keep the tension light.

Red and purple marle
slip stitches in a pattern
whose flow descends to cloth.

I work an ancient rhythm,
plied by the countless women
upon their stoops and hearths,
a tug of chords
which frees the heat,
my words had trapped inside.

Found Wanting

It is a wanton jinn
that grows and multiplies,
wild energy devoted to its seed.
In cult and law our stories wrought;
the sense they have to bring.

From chaos we divine
its reach outside our grasp.
Specks demanding light,
whose minds encompass galaxies
beyond their trembling sight.

Illusion

A mirror ball,
its many facets
flash and twirl.
We dance,
intoxicated by the noise,
of being on the floor
with those who share
our moves and speech,
the clothes we choose to wear.

Its glancing lights
reflect
the image we project,
exclude the truths
that don't belong,
of who we really are.
Prefer a light that spins
to keep us in the dark.

Metalworking

Ambition's forge has cooled,
its passion is a tempered blade
that I no longer crave.

Age cruels me of desire,
the only spark to burn
now sinters craft to dross.

I slump and oxidise
like metal, base as lead
which cannot be refined.

After the Funeral

For Helen 1945–2010

The lawyer and the will
are all that's left to do.
A handful of her things
a plastic bag or three,
a life, a death, an end
there wasn't much to show.

Our chapel was like her;
plain, discreet and small.
Lines of mourners grew,
then swelled to overflow.
She had surprised us all.
Her touch upon their hearts
more than we ever knew.

Powerless

My grief has blown
a fuse inside.
I sit, must rise and sit again
it's how the weeks descend.

No matter how I try to still
the twitching in my head
A thought appears,
then switches off
or trips and so expires.

This grief has not the power
to keep me slumped in bed.
It is a loss whose wiring
is shorting out the mind.

Had hoped in dreary cleaning
the cure I'd quickly reach,
but there's a limit to the wood
or glasses I can shine.

I've now resolved, just let it be
give in to restless ticks,
Will grab a lead and dog to tow
and walk till tiredness numbs.

Her Laughter

Laughter is a fingerprint
that holds the air we breathe.
It carries love and our surprise,
masks awkwardness and shame.

I think of her, the crinkled eyes,
mouth open in delight.
This is how the memory works
for those who we have loved.

The way her laugh
could lift you up,
the comfort it would bring.
Our world is all the poorer
in the silence of her heart.

As time distils
all she had been,
the laughter that she gave
still echoes in your own,
when you inhaled
the love she bore
a baby in her arms.

Trying

He lies
protection from
our angry blasts
frustrating life.

He tries
to act the man
struts, preens, big notes
tells all he can.

He lies
stained clothes askew
his features
not set right.

He tries
but cannot see
the dirty face
or smell he wears.

He lies
as words distort
in needs expressed
but mispronounced.

He tries
a child alone
and trapped inside
a loping grey-haired man.

Brother

You are a keening in my blood
no loud discord, you are a shadow,
who shifts according to the news,
reports of overdose or homeless deaths
are those that bring you close.

Beyond us now
where sharp wits and cunning rule,
on narrow streets for bed or worse
you'll find a church or musty stairwell
I saw it once and still I feel the wrench.

Bright red curls I envied in our youth
fade with the bond we shared.
An eager mind that always had a book
has found its universe
within the needle's hook.

Behind Locked Doors

The blade cuts slow,
inhale a stifled cry
then softly whimper to yourself.
Begin to rock forward and back
blood trickling down your thigh.
Another slice, it pulses out,
the wild intensity of pain.

Behind locked doors
old scars exposed and split apart,
it gives relief to cut
time and again.
Under your jeans the secret kept
from parents or a teacher's shock.

You have it all, good family,
home, bright future, friends,
expected to be grateful
but you're not.
The pointless, endless emptiness
is what you see.
Alone at night and with a knife
this pain you can control.

Icarus

In the free world of mania,
there are no inhibitions,
my mind is a street racer,
hot-wired for speed.

Music blasting in your face,
peacock hued, metallic bite.
Stigma has no hold on me,
at you I hurl its challenge.

Disregarding all the rules,
made for you pedestrians,
disapproval's high octane,
I'm pumping for attention.

My revs distort your cries;
bravura burning rubber.
I lose the wheel's control,
danger is my navigator.

The Game

Beyond polite facade,
appropriate disguise,
there is a greater need,
the secret self I guard.

Society insists
I choose a part
as pawn or knight,
so we can play the game.

I'll be discreet,
decipher codes
from evangelists
to media jocks
and those exploiting greed.

Deflect their spin
tune out excess
retain intact
the person deep within.

It's here I'm free
to measure and collect
the fragments of my past
in dreams I hold or grieve.

History

Shaped by misadventure
and secrets of the night
history will repeat itself
struggle as we might.

Hold us ever prisoner
in a silent pact
the spirit broken
by a random act.

Innocents abandoned
fear and guilt compound
no word is ever spoken
the circle tightly bound.

Child and man together
lost along the way
pain remains the constant
time will not allay.

Laos

Their jungle retches metal rain
into the streaming heat.
Rocks expose
where bombs have blown
the tops of hills
to ragged clumps,
the rest is closely grown.

A narrow bridge of track
cuts russet through the green,
a girl;
she does not know her age,
digs slowly in the dirt.

Since she could walk
each day she comes,
accompanies her sister
in the work,
they look for scrap to sell.

Lumps of shrapnel are
a never ending source
along the Ho Chi Minh.
Small hands know how
to gently ease
the twisted ends
of cluster bombs
nesting in the earth.

Slow work,
once farms grew crops,
but nowhere here is safe,
the land is rich
with unexploded ordinance.
She learns to concentrate,
with second sense moves
like a bird across the ground,
leaves suspect mounds alone,
runs home and tells the men,
red painted stick to mark
the place till others come.

They will defuse or
make these shells explode,
the girl hides underneath her house
and hums to block the sound,
tight fingers in her ears,
until the men have gone.
Next day her basket holds
a weight she cannot share.

Drones

And as we move apart,
impose a keyboard or a drone,
do you feel pain the less
from word or bomb,
the click of mouse
and shrapnel blast
if you are out of sight.
The lies we tell
are not caught out
when faces can't be read,
and distance builds a firewall
which no one can delete.

Running

My weakness for extremes,
desires transformation,
of cells eroding back
to join with tree and rock.

Born human, I can dream,
but always with a mind
that cleaves itself in two,
from highs to death wish lows,
this madness claims a toll.
Host of destructive genes
that link me with a past
I'm powerless to heal.

I wish to be reborn
as some wild water course,
that holds the flow of life
and runs upon our earth
without a need to dream.

What Cannot Be Contained

Each drop is absolute.
It falls through space,
holding life
and captured light.

Repeating out of time
beyond millennia.
It carves a chasm or a cave
within our rock and earth.

Locked into lakes
or swelling up from springs,
a river's course replenished
on melting ice.

We halt its pace
in tank and pipe
held tight for future use,
until the washer splits.

Each drop through space,
resumes the journey
as before,
against unyielding iron.

Eclipsing other sounds
it carves a chasm in my mind.
The silence broken by
a dripping tap
that cannot be contained.

Rot and Weeds

Old orchards left to rot and weeds,
sheds slumping to the ground.
The life that was will not return.
We want much more today.
Farms mean years of endless work,
no nightlife and poor pay.

With not enough to hold us here,
we leave them to decay.
The country with its open skies
is only worth a visit.
Clean air is something to enjoy
when briefly you are in it.

Now food is grown elsewhere,
out there,
where choice is not permitted,
comes shipped to us from overseas
demand led by their profits.

If all we eat comes in by air
what choice are we pursuing?
To kill our farms and not to care
the debts that we're accruing.

White Stone Blades

Eyes squint above the glare,
against dark gibber plains
bright quartz stands out,
stone tools lie scattered here.

A land of goat and hawk,
salt bush and weathered rock,
sand drifts to coat each one,
rejecting growth – tree sparse.

We shift to earth's slow curve,
the road's unbending clay
on flattened mountain range
at speed our timelines blur.

Solitary Confinement

A home that wraps her in
its density of green,
the quilt to keep her warm,
from all our worldly chills.

The child who planted trees
grew gnarled and strong
as her beloved groves of nuts
and orchard fruits.

The perfume she prefers
is compost with its heady notes
of worms and life's decay,
the herbs she brews for tea.

Her boundary's defined
by land she tills,
the rhythms of her hens
and chores that feed her day.

Hard work has made a lie
of the eighty years she claims,
eats what she grows,
no taste for life beyond
where grace does not belong.

Storm Thrush

Your plumage
dull as grey on grey,
a size to fit my hand.

And yet your song
has filled the sky,
in trills and warbles
for this bitter day.

Delight to give
your world a song
cascading
through my walls.
It draws me out
so I can sing
all that I find in you.

Unseasonal

The heart of every tree I loved
is broken to the ground,
their weight in years
spins out as woodchips,
chainsaws grind the air.

Tender leaves
made cradles for the snow,
piled up in minarets
to bend and drag limbs down.

Thaw reveals the damage done
with mulchers crowding streets.
Mother birds rebuild their nests
in trees split out of shape,
I garden with a saw
that's sharpened on our loss.

The Summer House

Vines twisted through a frame of mesh
grew dense enough to block the light,
a cool escape on humid days
it was our secret cave.

The heavy scented jasmine curled
with honey notes of clematis
whose seed pods twirled to
pompom balls around the spice
from climbing rose.
Then we had the storm.

We wait till petal-fall.
In heat and sweat we clip and hack,
among the thorns, seed pods and leaves
that cling to skin and clothes.
Bits of fluff work into mouths and eyes.
Peel back distorted wire and bough
a layered weight of green,
and tie the frame to trees.

Within the mess of our lost floor
we find a knot of twigs
with feathers from a breast.
It holds a tiny bird, now stiff and cold.
The mother could not reach her chick
when rain and snow caved in her home
and she was locked outside.

Reflecting on Monet

The flowers sown for love
now overwhelm my sanctuary.
The garden I conceived
has become a greedy muse,
I'm penned by fame.

Each day I rise
before it's light,
slip from the shore,
glide to the space where time
and thought dissolve.

Hands gnarled and stiff,
eyes blurred,
can still find shades,
cerulean, viridian,
the violets I desire.

My arm and brush
fuse at the wrist,
deft strokes will capture dawn,
transform the water's depth
to incandescent globes;
my lilies floating on
reflections of the sky.

Pure elemental marks,
each pigment I lay down
by instinct honed
as bees to pollen work,
before fatigue and cold
can shake me from the trance
which makes this painting scorch.

Blended in Blue

Like a sailor fresh on shore,
hair stiff with salt, my skin
set tight against sea gales,
I'm landed back and we
adjust to life as two.

Your mountain's air is chill
closed in by looming trees,
shrill parrots everywhere.
Fears of snakes or fires
are what the bush inspires.

Days drift and merge in weeks.
Tending to old chores,
we share our blend of love
as patterns shift or still.

We know that I must leave
when shades of sea invade.
Of your home I've made a port,
now crave the water's hue.

As we pull apart
our hearts will bond anew,
to the call of my home bay
you give me freedom's course.

Whale Watching

We gather on the cliffs
when winter days resume.
And look for signs
of breach or blowhole spray.

Dark weight beneath
warm water's buoyancy.
Bellies full of young
hold mothers to their course.

Males fuelled by potency
are following behind.
We count it luck to glimpse
a leap and splash of tail.

After the Storm

Light deepens to steel blue
upon a denser bay.

Night dusts its softer brush
on beachfront desolation.

Beauty found in broken things
thrown off an angry ocean.

Birds' wings and shattered fish
with coloured plastic shapes.

Shards scattered through the sand
or heaped above wave lines.

A jigsaw of our world
once whole and understood.

Storm's flung their sense apart.
among the bleaching kelp.

Art's made from our debris
that's tossed like empty shells
by us and churning seas.

Coastal

With a sigh your life is spread
in hungry sand's embrace.
You're bound to clasp the land
while held within the sea.

The past is honey gold
made of broken shells
in ochres, purple,
white and brown,
ancient rocks deposed
into mere grains.
forests cast as splinters
with fires' charred remains.

A speckled gull steps cautiously,
intent upon the heft of waves
plucks a living on the finds;
an urchin's heart
and bare scaffold
that once held up a fish.

Seaweed collects in arabesques
of grasses, ferns
and fingered hands,
a skein as fine as hair entwines
a strand of toad-skin pearls.

Shells like nubile breasts
are pale nipples to the sun
or turned upside,
small cups for offerings
of concentrated brine.

Coolum Morning

Awake in pre-dawn dark,
your soft breath
beside my ear.
I rise
and dress with stealth,
creep out the nearest door.

Slow step
towards the beach,
inhale
each bird's first call.
Warmth lingers in still air,
sand slips beneath my feet.

Rose fires break across the sky,
the ocean expands
with light.
Flames finger to the shore
and blaze
a river's mouth.

At Port

On Sunday afternoons
the noise which overlays
a coastal town,
falls mute.
Dogs look bored
and scratch imagined fleas.

Grey nomads
clutching fish and chips
retreat
to mobile homes
and satellite TV.

Stray walkers
slacken on their leads,
gaze past the river flats,
admire
the looping water threads
of dolphins leaving port.
Waves shuffle up the line
or silently disperse.

Tomorrow
shopping can resume,
and noise will bustle
through the streets,
to stores in loud display.

Calligraphy

Darkness
dissolves in ember hues.
The beach scoured clean,
no wind, just sky,
where an eagle drifts
then streaks away.
Sunrise reveals
calligraphic lines,
drawn by
the moving hand
of waves,
upon a parchment
of damp sand.

Shipwrecked

From moon's insistent pull
the motion of our blood
has ocean force.
Storm blast to harbour calmed,
all challenges
will test our sailing skill.

We prosper or decline,
the seasons fathom depth
until we find
our own devouring wave
to sweep us
into the heart's whirlpool,

to surge or drown
in love's wild undertow
shipwrecked and
entwined.

Teasing

Soft days tease
towards the spring
doves harvest twigs.
In camouflage of fallen leaves
their males display.
A butcher bird lands
by my hand, perhaps
it waits for gifts of food.

A graceful carpet snake
manoeuvres past our chair,
insinuates within the roof
above my head,
until it's warm enough
to seek another's nest to share.

Painting Lives

Shift and hold today
move through its moments slowly.

The pace of life discounts
our senses and their meaning.

These instants form a stain
whose colour will remain

to paint your life intensely.

The Quiet

Within a world of silence
there is no Mozart to explore,
no accents for our words.
We cannot hear the ocean roll
or our beloved calling.

We are enclosed,
there is a cushion on our lives,
where scent or taste or touch
can never compensate
for just one sound
that sets our hearts to leaping.

www.ingramcontent.com/pod-product-compliance
Lightning Source LLC
Chambersburg PA
CBHW062205100526
44589CB00014B/1955